It's not the World that's Fragile

that's Fragile

- it's us

J S Langley

Print ISBN: 978-1-8380177-2-9

For my long-suffering wife Janet, our children-now-men, Robert, Iain and Michael, their partners Sophie, Laura and Kirst, and our grandchildren Abbie, Benjamin and James …

… and particularly to Iain for use of his original artwork.

Contents

It's not the World that's Fragile

J S Langley

Getting to Here

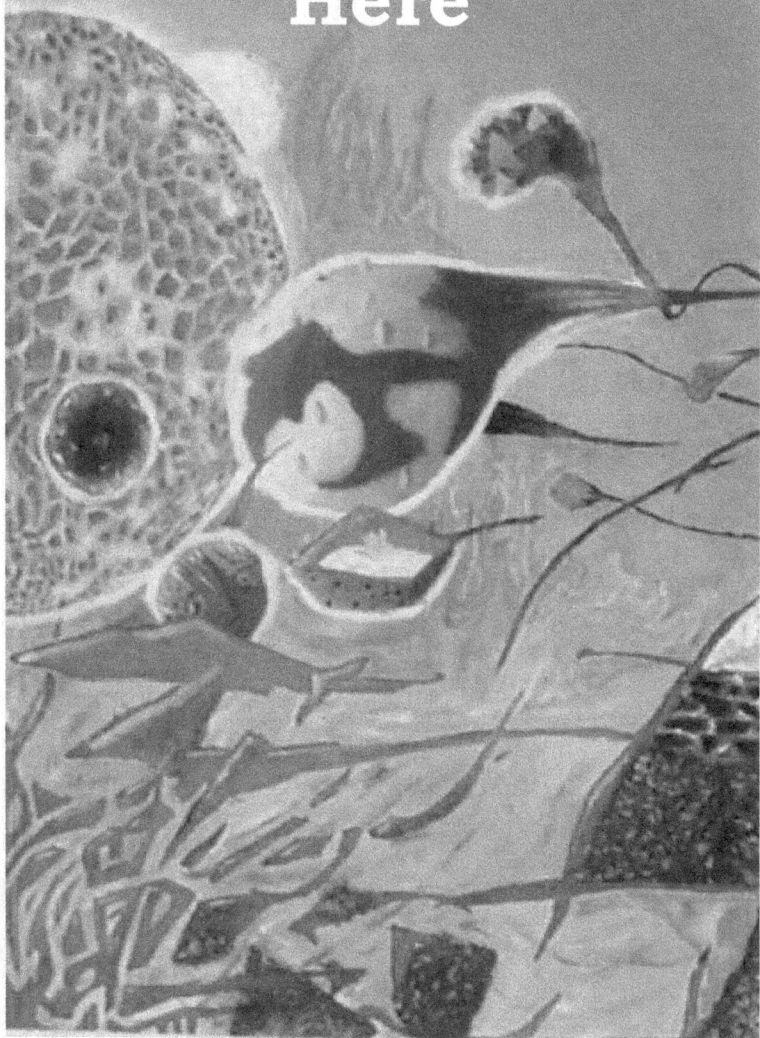

A Quirk in the Cosmos

a cloud of hydrogen and little else   bereft of light
in the silence of space   rippled from uniformity
by waves of radiation   interstellar winds
the wake of galaxies

mass moves to mass   disturbances increase   creating
topography   darkness collapses into darkness
driven onwards into itself   in its own good time.

Accretion accelerates accretion   proximity develops
pressure   temperatures rise   a spark   an ignition
and nuclear fusion kicks in - births a new star

that begins to emit its own energy spectrum   gamma
X-ray   ultra-violet   infrared   microwave   radio   and
(less than a millionth of one percent of all its wavelengths)

that which will become visible light   carried by photons   fed
by chain reactions   ready to give sight to future eyes
evolved to see.

***

Around the star   a disc
the attracted dust of long dead stars

its myriad parts swarm   amidst magnetic lines
colliding   clumping   sorted by elemental fundamentals
into bands   waves   strands that stick together.

Piece on piece planetesimals grow
and clear a way through   mopping up mass
some become large enough for internal external forces
to push and pull   inwards   outwards   moulding matter

into a sphere   developing a core   that radiates heat
convects   conducts   differentiates into layers   becomes
a new thing; proto-planet
that continues to accrete
and this one
this one
suffers collision
and forms a companion moon an 80th the size of itself
that settles into synchronous orbit.

***

It's not the World that's Fragile

Molten the planet
flexes volcanically rotates
develops a magnetic field that
deflects high energy particles squeezes
out layers of gas. Sound is born. A cooling
world slithers slowly towards a slender range
of temperature where water, released from
minerals and comets flows   fills chasms basins
balances tides that wash the shores of new land
that emerges   rises   erodes   is wind-swept rain-
washed forms pools in which bio-reactions can
repeatedly   occur   and   in   this   crucible
this earth   this air   this fire   this water - life.

A succession of bacteria plants fish reptiles
mammals insects that can see   hear   smell
taste   touch   can sense   themselves are
self-selected through opportunity   chance
circumstance co-evolution is inextricably
intertwined in interconnected interdependent ecosystems, math-
ematical, chemical, physical processes… a biospheric melting
pot in which each era seems complete permanent to its
own inhabitants though each one is superseded
life upon life laid down layer upon layer
irregular regularity of formation.
A quirk in the cosmos dictated
by simple common laws
each outcome unique
like snowflakes.
One new snowflake
immersed in a universe
of other unique snowflakes.

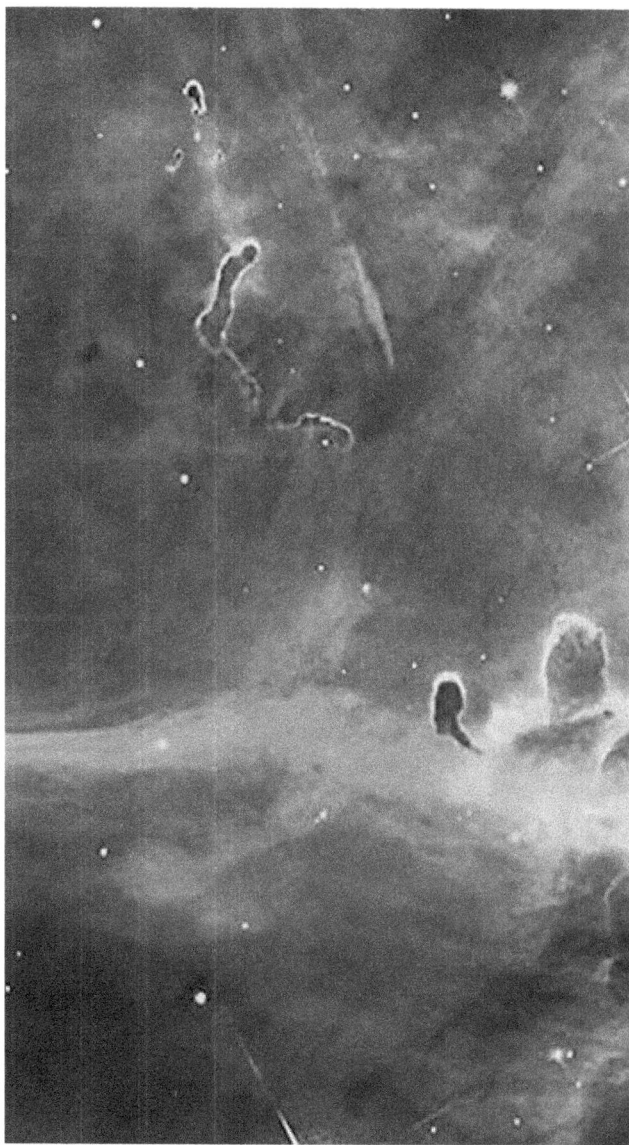

A Convoluted Track-way

On a wobbling Earth, that does not yet know its name
whose tilt varies, whose orbit fluctuates in
eccentricity, stromatolites thrive though they poison
their own atmosphere, their breath filled with
toxically exhaled oxygen

> essential for other forms of life, interconnected
> roots & branches on the one tree that grows as
> water drips, from giant fronds, swayed by the
> passing of large beasts, the pull of prehensile
> tongues that reach to tear and taste unaware

of a bright free falling fireball
that flames impartially in a rush to end
a 200 million year era in a single event
plunging, precipitating a radical review
with no appeal...

***

Around 5 million years ago a permutation
in a rift valley produces a larger brain that proceeds
(in another million years) to reach a half a litre and
continues to grow, coincident with global
climate change.
The number of sub-species increase,
reduce, then spread along migratory paths
in step with the Neanderthals, together for 150,000 years.

***

It's not the World that's Fragile

All now left are members of the same subspecies, our lives regulated
by the rotation of the Earth, the rhythms of light and dark.
Inhabiting a world of fresh water, that makes up
sixty percent of our body mass

Bodies
containing digestive bacteria, honed to our diet of fat, proteins
and carbohydrates

Metabolisms that
break down then manufacture enzymes, hormones, bone
and blood

Standing
on our own two feet, believing we are in control

Knowing that
the Earth does not mourn the dinosaurs
- and neither do we.

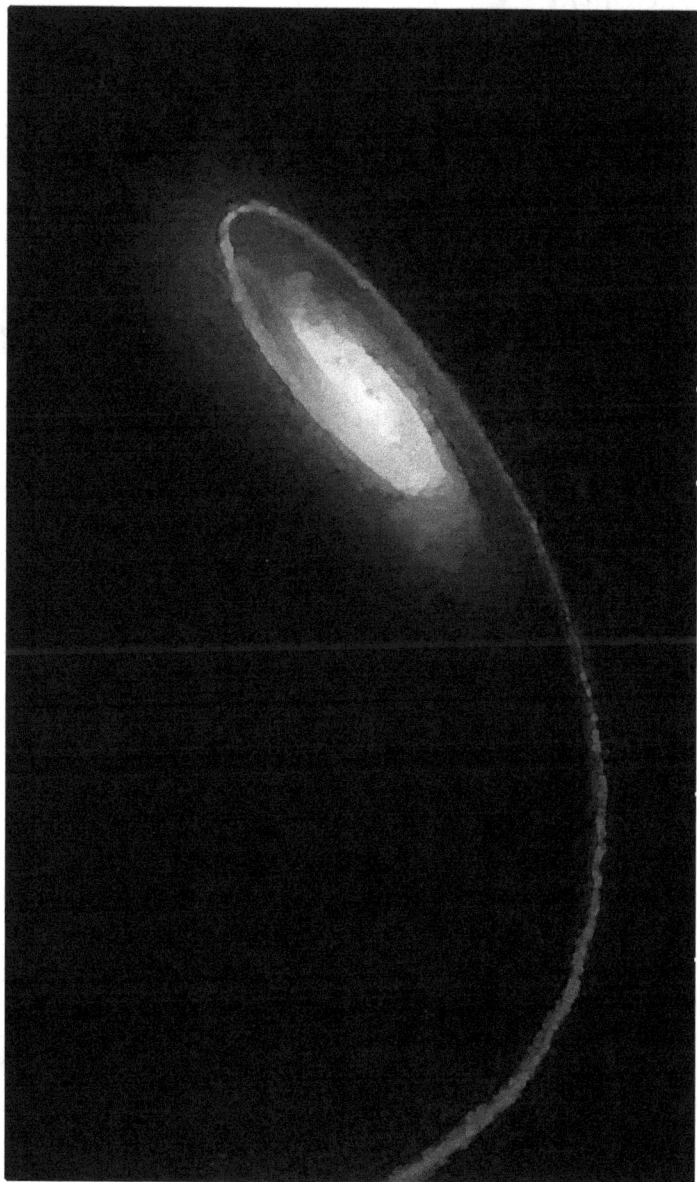

The Spear
and the Flame

Blessed.
Fruitful. Social.
Omnivorous. Creative.
Dominant.   Intelligent.
Talkative. Dexterous. A big
brain protected in a bone shell
that contains as many neurones
as   there are stars in a   galaxy.

***

In a cave   an artist   hunter   butcher
smelling of cooked meat the fragrance
of fruits and damp leaves fingers tipped
in red ground ochre mixed with animal grease
smears marks on a warm night eyes intent under
a flickering yellow flame   on a smooth cave wall
We were here

This is what we did
and other faces look on heads nod in comprehension
at matchstick figures drawn up in a semi-circle facing
a large horned beast throwing their sharp-tipped spears
enough hitting home to know that the wait will not be
long before the skin can be cut away the meat sliced
into pieces and carried home. The fresh grease on their
chins is proof of a successful hunt security in
a huddled group
gives hope of
a good night's
sleep.

Dexterity

Cult-

-iva-   -tion   cat-

-ches   on;   wheat

barley   peas   lentils

fuels   settle-   -ments   home-

-steads   keep-   -ing   goats

gives   time   to look   into the   far

night sky   for   patterns of   meaning   or   portents

and ways to control the rain.   Ritual   culture

aural   histories are   offspring of   their   fertile minds

their   dexterous fingers   their god-given   means

to tear down or build   to pray   or   to persecute

to   cup water   and drink   to touch   to feel.

The hand   the eye   the brain   the   first

trinity   harnessed   extended

holding forth

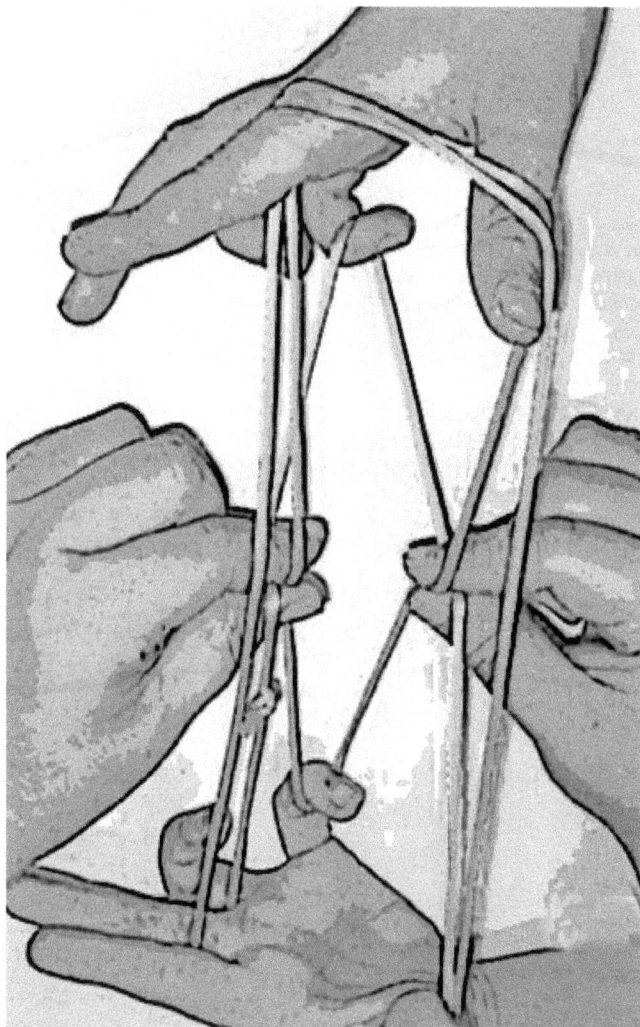

What is Writ

Voice, listening, learning by doing
allows passage of ideas until symbols
chipped or scratched or scrawled
become the written word coursing
through the bloodstream
of collective memory

spreading error spreading truth
building a thoroughfare of thought
from the dead to enable the living
to exist in all three worlds
past, present and future
at the same time.

Each new generation learns
from the last
Euclid to Galileo
Kepler to Newton to Maxwell
to Einstein - ideas that last
longer than civilizations

that lie beneath our feet
their bare remains unearthed
as chance dictates and pondered on
by prying eyes that gaze
searching for lost memories
in these cracked mirrors.

And what is not writ (or writ and lost) is found and lost
and found again or lost and lost...

Outreach

We are a species that has traveled beyond our world and walked upon the Moon leaving bootprints. That has launched a probe into space and thirteen years later has given it an instruction to turn around and look back across nearly four billion miles of space and take a photograph of our Home that fills less than a pixel a pale blue dot.

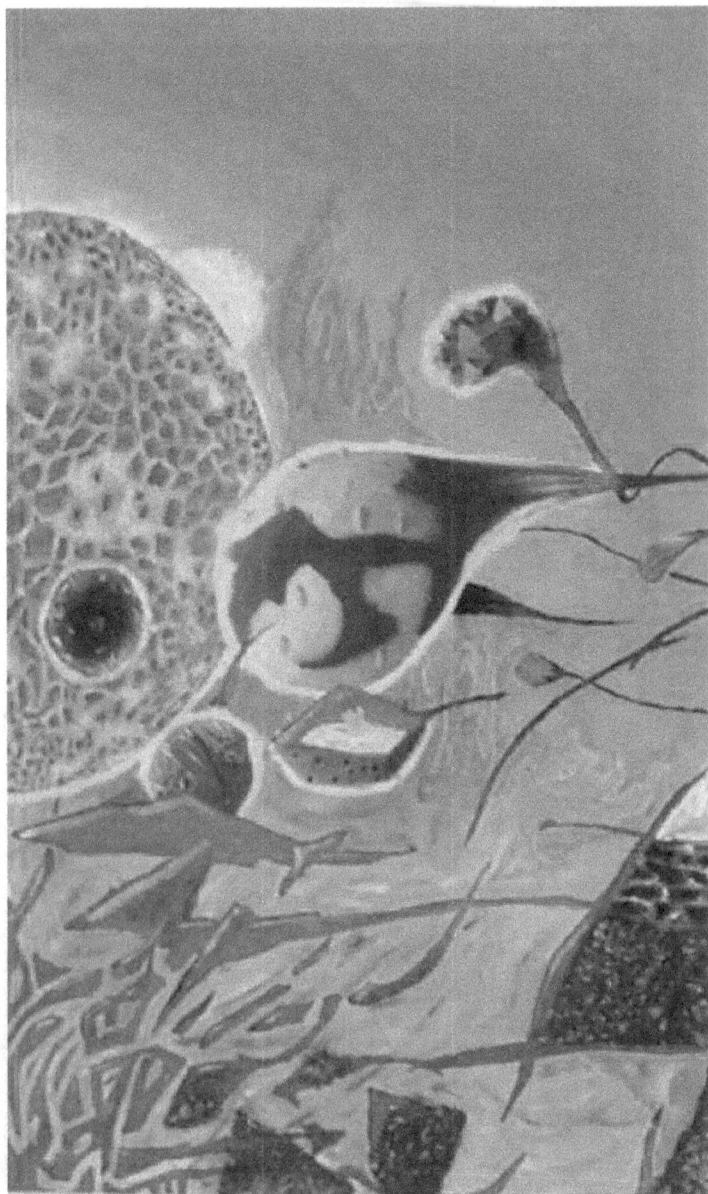

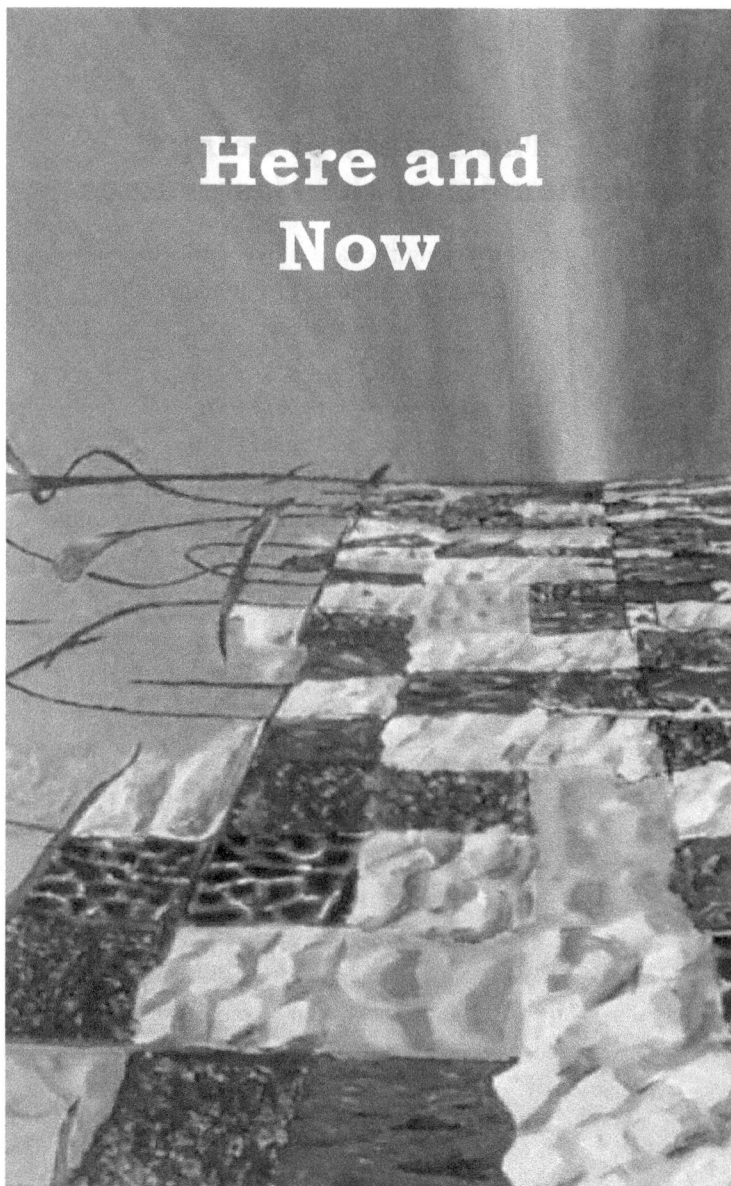

Here and Now

The Beauty of Being
a Member of the Master Race

... is believing the race is over and won
… is having the weapons to dominate all
other species
… is farming
genes for the best flavour
or speed … is taking command of the
elements; Earth   Air, Fire   and Water
to do with   as we wish.   … is exploiting
the seemingly   boundless   bounty that is
at our fingertips.   … is being superior   by right
believing   this right   is ours
forever.   … is assuming   the power
to burn down   rainforests   (without the
problem of   responsibility).   … is harbouring
the ambition   to satisfy   every want.
Things as simple and as
guilt-free as
a morning coffee
palm oil soaps
bananas, mangoes, fresh tomatoes all year round.
Surely this is not too much to ask – for Members of the Master Race.

24

Surviving in the Age of Numbers

We did not know, how could we
what the results would be
when we invented numbers
and counted 1, 2, 3

10

So simple was the method
so helpfully sublime
how could we know what numbers
would come to mean in time

9

From barter to a number
the value of a hen
a pig, a horse, a mattress
trade was simple then

8

But we began to value
the numbers we could hold
and fought to own the images
in silver, bronze and gold

7

The numbers came to rule us
deciding what we'd do
even Nature was a number
Our own value too

6

Outside the waters are rising
forests burn, starvation grows
while we sit by our firesides
ignoring what's under our nose

5

1......2......3... 4...

Imminent Threats
mean Nothing to Us

Really
we are so clever
we can clean up our air
our old rivers, we can even
close a hole in the ozone layer.

We prolong our lives by
removing threats.

Even invisible enemies we fight and overcome
but now it seems we're being conspired against by;

Rain that burns.
Water that poisons.
Food that refuses to grow.
Tablets that no longer cure.
Plastics that choke our waterways.
Oils that leak. Fires. Floods. Hurricanes.
Words not spoken.   Action not taken.
Consequences not   clearly understood.
Changes not made   (in good time).
Language used to confuse. Distractions used to delay.
One
set of threats
traded for
others.
What could we have done to deserve this?

Mask

Made from past pieces pulped hurt held joy coloured days
I am the mask covering hiding thoughts emotions too raw
to expose to   the world unfiltered   You hide inside
peeping through   I am your mask   pliable to the task
                       choose me wisely
                       today for business
                       tonight a parent
                       partner
                       lover
                    I am them all
at your beck and call masking the vulnerability
    of your feelings   always available
        never prying   into what lies
          beneath what   really matters
              I have a job to do.
              I do it well.

How Sides Come Together

'We are continuing to
pump greenhouse gases
into the atmosphere. At
this rate temperatures will
rise by 2 degrees
within the next 15 years.'

*'But how do we know
this to be true?'* asks the
skeptical politician.

'We have modeled
the Physics, the Chemistry
the Biochemistry, built
and tested algorithms
simulated multiple scenarios.
All these show this is the best
we can expect to happen.'

'The best?' queries the
spokesperson for the
fossil fuel industry.

'The least developed part
of our model concerns
possible feedback loops
runaway reactions. For example
increasing temperatures
will begin to defrost Siberian
permafrost, releasing quantities
of methane which will increase
the temperatures further
and faster, melting more
releasing more
heating faster etcetera, etcetera.'

*'So there are uncertainties
in the modelling?'* asks
a journalist.

A moment of quiet. The air holds its breath.

'There are always
uncertainties
in some areas, but…'

'So nothing is 100% guaranteed.
You could be wrong,' says
the decision-maker.

'We may be imprecise
but the direction is clear.
It's down to the Laws of Nature.'

'Empirically developed,'
asserts the climate change
nay-sayer.

'The Growth Economy,
built on extract-use-discard
could not go on forever.'

'You could be wrong,
You've already admitted there are
uncertainties,' repeats the chorus.

'But…'

'Thank you. We will need to think about
the Economic, Political and Social
repercussions. It is all very complex.
It may take us some time,'
says the chairperson
to nods of approval.

It's not the World that's Fragile

'And in the meantime?'

*'In the meantime please return
to your laboratory and keep
improving your models.
Work on removing
all the uncertainty
then come back
and see us again.
We are very
appreciative
of your efforts.
Thank you,
that is
all.'*

Miles Apart

'Come on now, you're getting in the way,'   says the Policeman in riot gear
stooping and starting to remove
the superglue.

'Why here, why now?'   ask the Commuters, trying to push
past and reach the Underground Station
because they're going to be late for work.

'How long will you keep on?'   asks the Journalist, a microphone
in her hand

*'Do you think it's right to inconvenience
the general public like this? What have
they done to you? Where do you come
from, what is your story, is there nothing
else you could be doing? It's starting to rain.
How much longer can you keep this up?'*

'I believe in the principle of peaceful protest,'   says the Politician, precisely
dressed, speaking into camera

*'but there are limits. I'm not saying we've
reached them yet. Freedom of speech is
something I hold very dear.'*

'Into the van,'   says the Policeman
'we gave you a chance...

     ...you just wouldn't listen.'

LEAVE IT IN THE GROUND

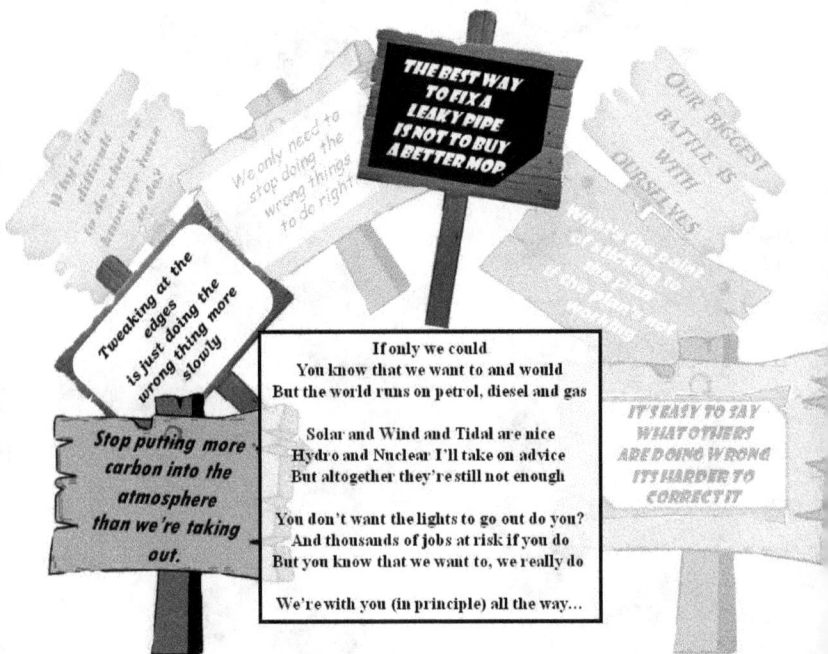

THE BEST WAY
TO FIX A
LEAKY PIPE
IS NOT TO BUY
A BETTER MOP

OUR BIGGEST
BATTLE IS
WITH
OURSELVES

We only need to
stop doing the
wrong things
to do right

Tweaking at the
edges
is just doing the
wrong thing more
slowly

Stop putting more
carbon into the
atmosphere
than we're taking
out.

IT'S EASY TO SAY
WHAT OTHERS
ARE DOING WRONG
ITS HARDER TO
CORRECT IT

If only we could
You know that we want to and would
But the world runs on petrol, diesel and gas

Solar and Wind and Tidal are nice
Hydro and Nuclear I'll take on advice
But altogether they're still not enough

You don't want the lights to go out do you?
And thousands of jobs at risk if you do
But you know that we want to, we really do

We're with you (in principle) all the way…

Who

Clothes sizes are getting artificially small
they're meant for someone twice as tall
It's not you

Temperatures are rising producing a sweat
some people are starving but I'm willing to bet
It's not you

The seas are dying they just cannot cope
being filled up with plastics that I only hope
Is not yours

We seem to be suffering blow after blow
who can do anything 'cos we all know
It's not you

We did nothing
wrong

When there was time to do something

we smiled, nodded in all the right places

AND

consulted our smartphones to ensure

we were doing nothing
wrong

Glutting

After the crowds had gone the gulls came
flocking raucously, fighting over
scraps

feasting on discarded food; chips, buns, burger bits,
battered fish, ripping open the crisp wrappers, punching
through polystyrene lids with determined beaks

mobbing each other, robbing from full mouths, filling
the air with shrill cries only they understood. Screeching,
bloating their bellies

knowing such abundance is fleeting, that this
glutting can not last   must not last will not last
forever.

It's not the World that's Fragile

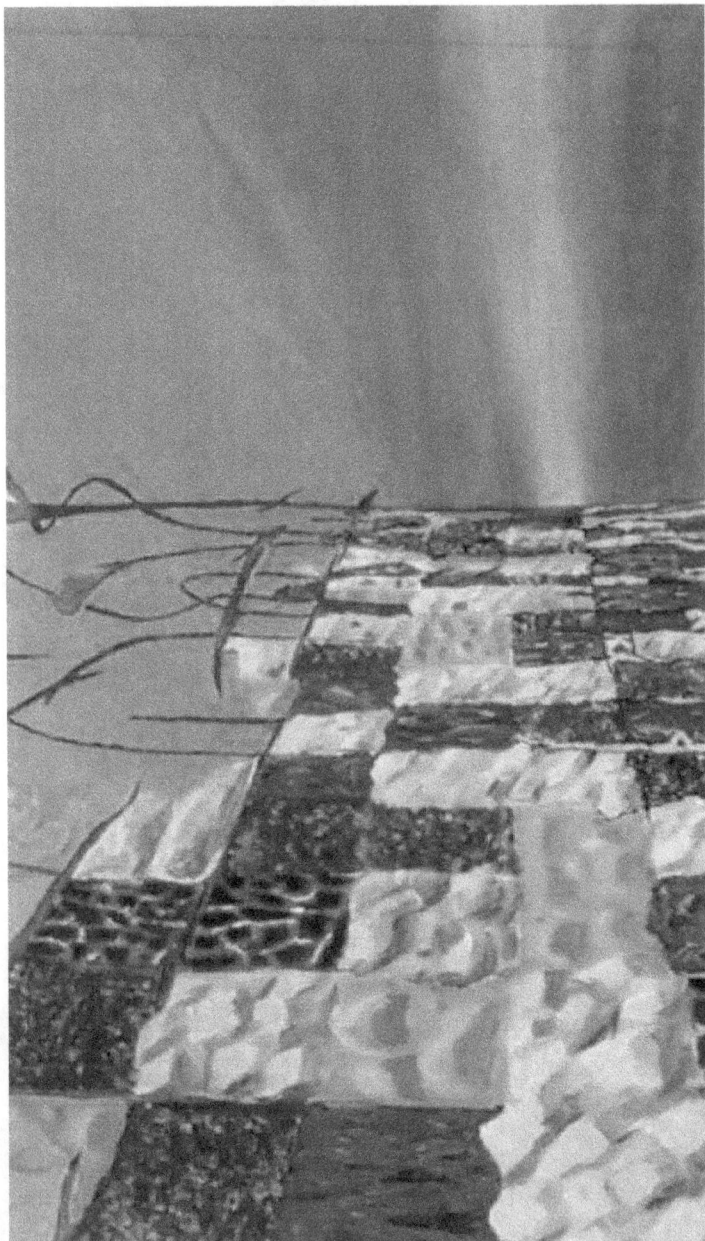

J S Langley

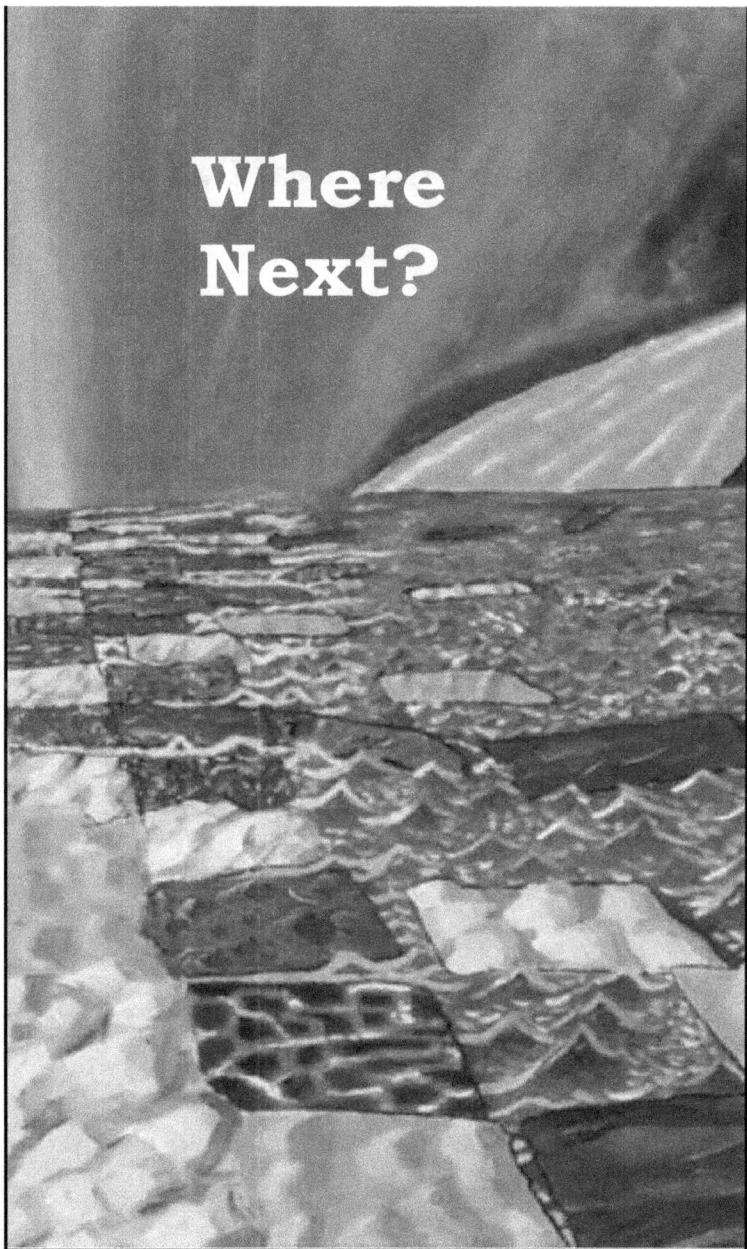

Where
Next?

Listening with Deaf Hands

Do we only need to listen
to know the things we need to change?
For far too long we haven't learnt

       the lessons. Listening to the little
       people, all the people, with a range
       of views is what we need to do.

              Listening to their words, their life
              stories, their ideas however strange
              will reveal to us our better selves
              that for too long we haven't heard.

       Learning lessons so we can look
       forward, on the basis of interchange.
       What we need to do is listen.

If we don't listen, learn the lessons,
the things we know we need to change
for far too long we haven't learnt

will stay undone. So you'll be pleased to know that we intend to listen.
    It's a big job. We can't wait to start the exchange of views.
      What we need to do is listen. For far too long
        we haven't learned.

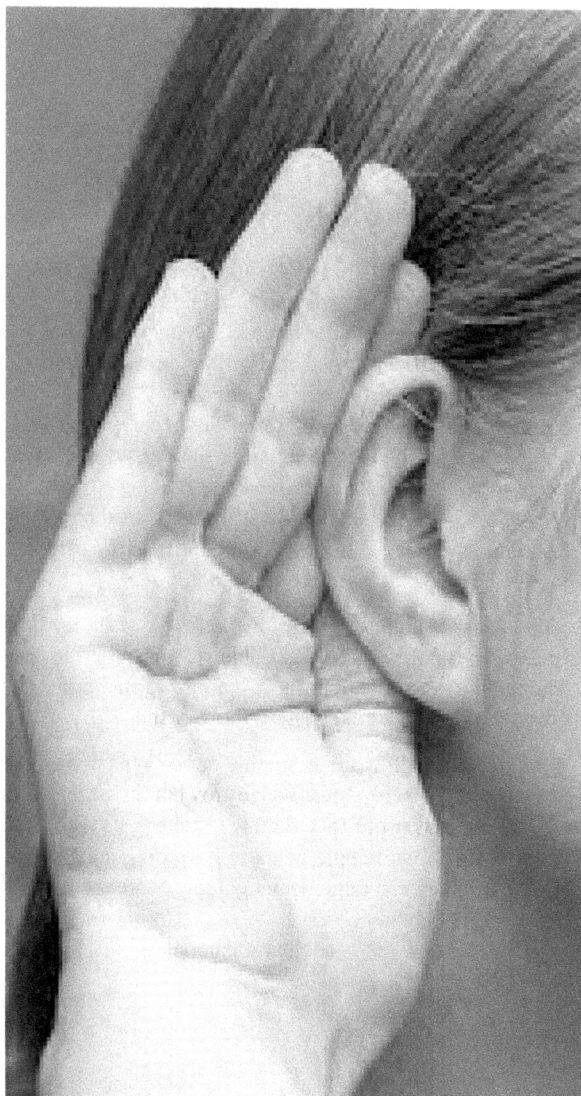

The Inconsiderate Enemy

How do you
fight against something
that does not fight back? That
simply stands, absorbing the blows,
changing colour, predictably unpredictable,
scientifically speaking, without sentience, with-
out emotion.
Something that deals out its own consequences as
inevitable as the sun crossing the sky, with no plans
for the future. How does intelligent biology w ar with
physics and che mistry when they are at odds with air th-
at cannot be seen, water that cannot be held, e arth that can-
not be heard, fire t hat dare not be felt...

Who wins? Who has always won? We can read it from
the rocks, the fossils, po s sible futures buried in past lives
though we spend the deposit ed past to fuel our own prog-
ress, our dreams of everlasting gro wth.

We pass through while hastening our o wn passing. Do we
not enjoy it here? Must we destroy all in order to rule
supreme over our own demise? Like gods who destr-
oy their own temple, who rel ease dragons they th-
ink they can tame, leaving only scorched bon-
es behind
as their memorial.

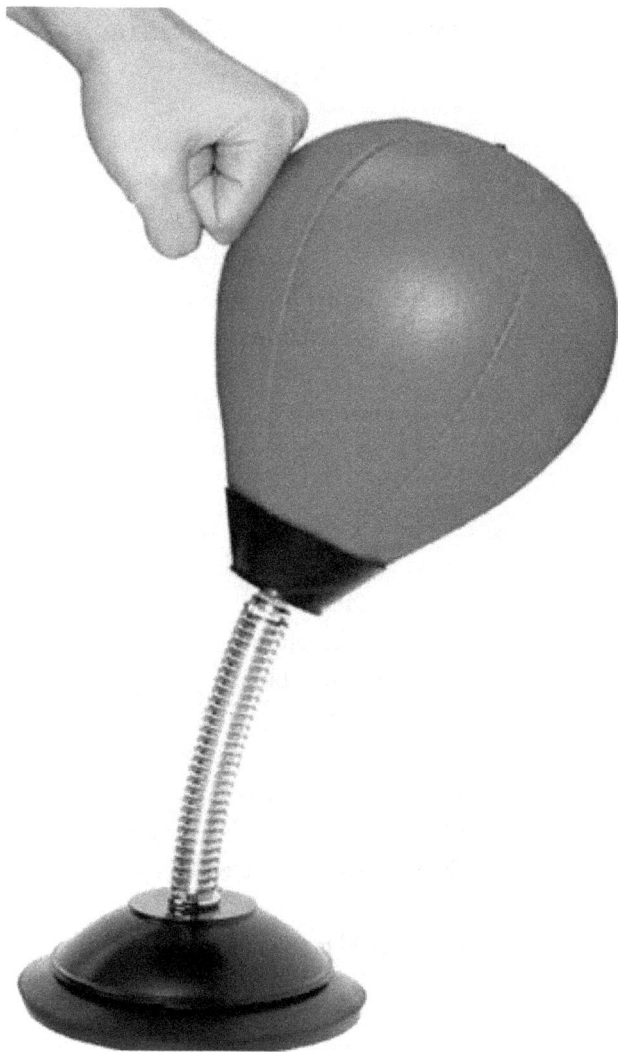

What we do in a Crisis

When is
a fire is too big to put out
a wave too big to outrun
a land too degraded to grow

**There   must be   someone
to blame**

Surely heads must roll someone must reap
what so many have sown

There must be a reason we got things wrong
a head   must fall a demi-god be forced to
resign and take the walk of shame suffer
humiliation   on behalf of   us all   before
disappearing from public   view   to
somewhere   warm   and   retiring.

While   we hear of people starving
While   we watch   the fires   burn
While we see   the waters surge

That should get things moving.

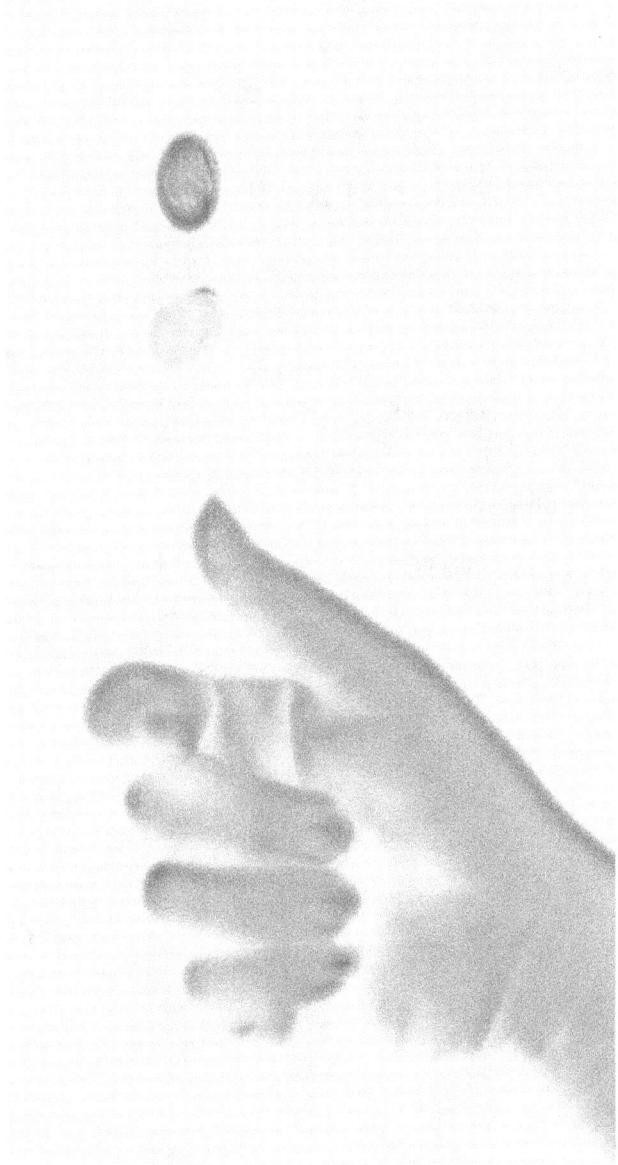

Point of No Return

Could we see it coming? Maybe
...in 5 years   ...in 15 years   ...in 30 years

So we knew we had to act
...now   ...in the next 5 years   ...in the next 20 years

It's just a shame that
the scientists...   the politicians...   the media..

even though we knew how to move to a new economy
Use   Reuse   Regenerate

could not agree on anything except the need for
more data
more talking
more waiting...

If only they had turned around, or glanced over their shoulder
they might have seen the point of no return
was already behind us.

Remains

Beneath the husk of earth I lie waiting
sanctified by the passing of what I once was
the people, rituals, beliefs, the market places
full of butchered meats, farmed vegetation.

Find my bare bones hidden within the recovering
green of forests, buried deep in churned and freshly
consecrated rain-washed soil and wind-blown sands.
Look upon me again ye mighty diggers in your search

for lost worlds that can be conquered, pillaged, with
only a shovel, the flowing sweat of hired brows, sneaking
treasures away under shawls, in pockets, wondering
what I once was, when and how and who, at a safe distance.

Look into my mirror, see yourselves. Do you not think
we believed ourselves immortal? Do you not consider
that we thought we were the pinnacle of creation that
now lie beneath your feet… sanitised… and cleansed.

Dinosaur Footprint

A
single
foot. It is
twice the size
of my hand
frozen in mud
-rock   an unknown   beast
from   another time   a different
but same   world   forms a
hollow that   holds today's   cold rain

How was this   footfall made?   On what day
did this   animal   pass by
thinking   its thoughts   being itself?

I put down my bare hand and wince as the
water spreads icily between my fingers.
I close my eyes try to make
a connection

Fail.

I know that any trace I may leave
behind me is unlikely to last as
long as this. On the slow walk
back to the car I look, like
Buzz Aldrin, for soft
forgiving patches of
impressionable
ground.

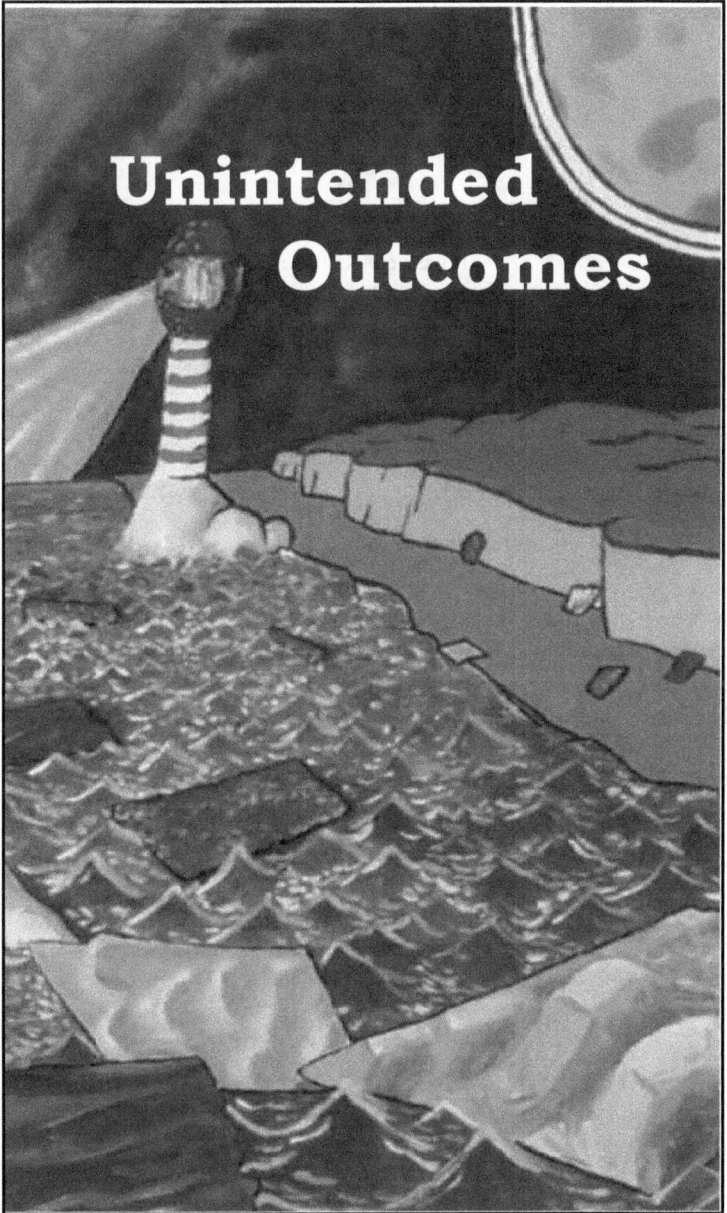

Unintended Outcomes

Ironic

If we were no longer here
there would be no protests or
task forces, no endless political debates

over the cost of change, if things could be fixed more cheaply *Money would not exis*

over who told the truth and who dealt in lies *It would be all too clea*

over how quickly things needed to be done to be in time *It would be too la*

over who is to blame and how they should be punished *It would not matt*

over why we didn't manage to invent a way out *We will not have do*

Here is irony… if soon we were not here there would be no more fossil fuels ripp
from beneath the ground to burn. No more industrial gasses polluting the atmosphe
No more plastics filling the sea and the bellies of fish. Grass would grow over tarma
Trees would branch uncut. Skyscrapers would be new homes for raptors seeking clif
The species decline would be reversed. CO_2 levels drop. All the things we should
have done to protect ourselves would be achieved by our absence.
New and different oxygen breathing species would thrive and
maybe, millennia later, our fossilized remains would be found
and pondered over by new academics
who would wonder how we looked
whether we had fur or feathers
walked on four legs or two
what happened to us
and when
and how. Here is irony

Bonfire in the Night Time

You take my hand and we walk into a vision of what may or may not be.
It is dark. The streets are full of broken glass and scattered DNA.
At a blazing fire are gathered hunched figures and stray dogs.
Barking.   Crackling.   Smelling   of damp clothes   damp dogs.

A man a white man in a torn suit approaches disheveled his pockets
stuffed full.   His lips move.   His face is dirty bruised. He appeals
for help holds out handfuls of notes. Two of the faces around the fire
look up while a mother and child huddle together close to the flames.

His notes are taken his jacket stripped from his back and thrown
onto the fire   where it moulders   giving off little heat.
The man cries.   We hear   words

> *Not my fault   I was doing what*
> *I thought was right   to look after myself.*

Those round the fire turn their backs.
The man attempts to join them…
creeps closer
to the warmth.
They close ranks
decades too late   they close
ranks in unison   saying nothing.

The last we see   is the man
        now without
                his jacket
                    his white shirt
                        no longer white
                            his white face
                                smeared black
                                    shoulders shaking
                                        as he
                                            disappears
                                        into
                                    the
                                broken
                        dark.

It's not the World that's Fragile

Around the bonfire the people begin to chant
It's not my fault

The Twist in the Tale

Searching with the expectation
of finding answers
inventions, cures, or antidotes.
Some last minute revelation
leading to a total resolution.

This is our belief: we can always find
a way out. Like detectives we follow
the clues and on the final page
there is always a solution.

Here is the twist in this tale
the twist in this tale is that …

there is no twist in the tale.

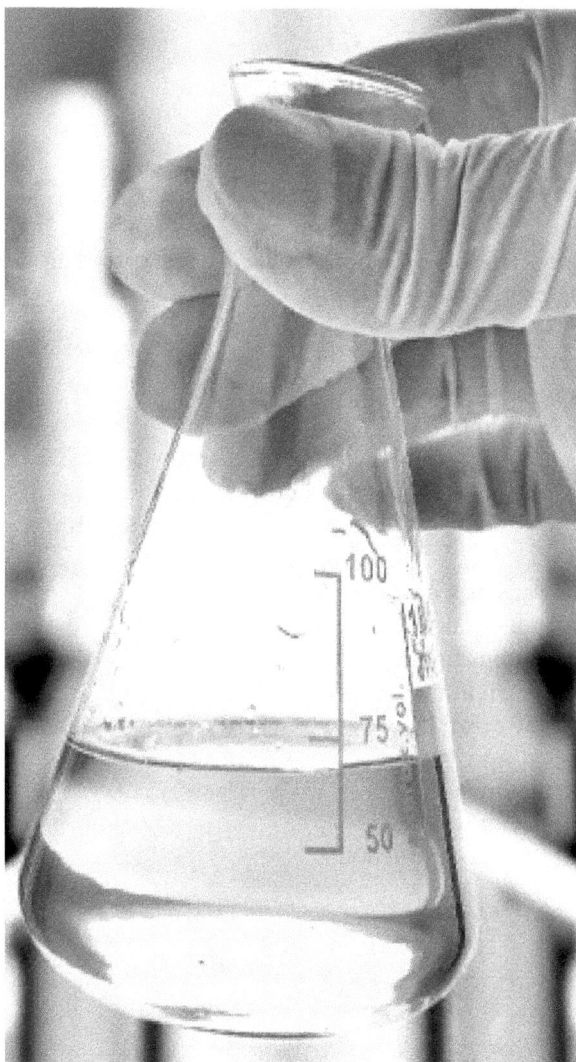

New World

Doomsday crept over the horizon like a duvet spreading silence
wrapping protest in swan down.

Disinterested in the falling sleepers
the buildings crumbled
beyond complaint
                beyond discourse
                            beyond currency
                                        into earth.

The final war was a mistake
a twitchy trigger finger and reprisals
desperate nations fighting over scarce resources
destroying them in the process
hastening their own demise.

I saw the bloom
        felt the hot breath
                of self-destruction.

Walking the Shoreline after a Storm

Pieces of lives dredged back into light
charred pages of burned books
piles of seaweed   bladders drying to husks
that crunch underfoot
driftwood layered at the reach of the tide

***

There are still more microbes in a spoonful of soil
than there are people on the planet.

***

After the tsunami I walk through what is left.

Houses broken into sticks   cars lifted   rolled   turned
remnants scattered bodies stranded   piled in stink.
Earth air   fire   and water   remain
but not for us.

***

J S Langley

I hear my breathing   rasping through valves   in
out   in   through a protective face mask. Tanks
beep on my back   built for lightness. Before my eyes
the holographic monitor tells me the time left

before I must retreat into the protected indoors

away from the high energy rays that now pass through
the damaged atmosphere
full of holes.

***

It's not the World that's Fragile

I pick up a piece of driftwood
old   smoothed   channelled   with
fossilised tunnels of dead sea-worms   from
an earlier   unpolluted sea - where there were fish
before the salinity rose too high   before chemicals

plastics   radiation   undermined the tree
ate at the roots
felled the edifice
left me to walk the tidelands a little longer
until the air filters saturate or
until the clouds part
and the sun comes out.

Saying Goodbye

I fly above the dry wreck-scattered seas
Under the hum of my engines
the fuel gauge flutters into the red
as mountains rise and my descent begins

kicking dry sand into clouds of held heat
I take her down gently on four metal feet

The hiss of the door, the sound of my boots
My suit protects me from the poisonous air
heavy to wear amidst such absolutes
of hot and cold and the searing glare

I tread on hard ground, my sole leaves no mark
and voices call from out of the dark
blown by the wind past my metal hood
What have we done? It is no good

in the parched land my mind plays a trick
I hear an answer '*I am beautiful in your death*'
My gloved hands reach up to make the catch click
My visor opens and I take a breath.

How Change Happens

Beginning as a single spring, strong thrusting
   mineral laden, clear, not frightened to
      be cold and chatter among the unheeding

rock

     and trickle down through temperamental beds
       worn by rains, the water rising, falling, gather-
       -ing like-minded runoff, seepage, stream
       joining to stream, the old

path

      not followed, but another gouged out
   of the status quo, dug deep, by protesting
 feet, running rapids, sharp sided crevass-
  -es, ignoring the calls to slow down to

pool

    to lake or loch or lough, to reservoir
   to be dammed, to pause, dashing on instead
  to deepen through widening banks, birthing a river
that threads a new course, a new norm, and in the reed beds

slows

because the time is right to wander, sift, mingle, merge a mix of
different waters that join, separate, stir up, turn over the turbulence
of new beginnings prepare and become recognized as bein
and then proceed after this tortuous journey onward in

surge

ready   to   rise   in   waves   filled with the   powe
to   get things   done   new   things   full of   fresh
water   rising up   to   quench   old   thirsts
until   the   next   course   change

the next spring rising

It's not the World that's Fragile

J S Langley

Notes on visual content

Getting to Here

p.6   *A Quirk in the Cosmos* – The poem develops spatially from chaos until we encounter the egg motif – a metaphor that appears in many creation stories.

p.18   *What is Writ* – Although the poem image is a book to give familiarity the first known written word was cuneiform script, created in Mesopotamia, present-day Iraq, ca. 3200 BC as shown in the accompanying illustration.

p.20   *Outreach* – The image represents the Voyager 1 mission that took a photograph of the Earth from a distance of 3.7 billion miles on Feb 14 1990 (Valentine's Day).

Here and Now

p.24   *The Beauty of Being a Member of the Master Race* - The root derivative of the symbol Φ (phi) is 'divinely-animated-entity'.

p.26   *Surviving in the Age of Numbers* - represents an overall countdown in a world full of, and obsessed with, numbers.

It's not the World that's Fragile

Where Next? - Each poem in this section contains a question - reflecting the uncertainty in the section's title.

Unintended Outcomes

Poems with Graphics

'What is writ' (book), *'Leave it in the Ground'* (placards), *'The Twist in the Tale'* (ebook) are linked by the use of the written word.

'Outreach' (spacecraft), *'Entering the Age of Numbers'* (flowchart), *'Remains'* (spade) are linked by the idea of 'progressing in one direction whilst looking back in another'.

Note: One of the thematic verbal links across all four sections are the primeval elements; Earth, Air, Fire, Water … immersed in the fifth all-pervading element – Time.

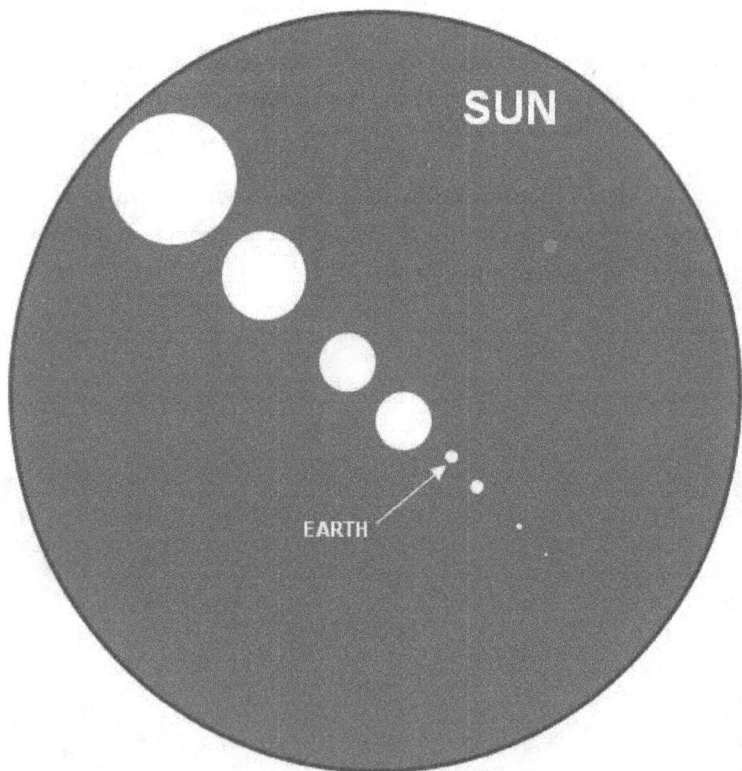

About the Author

John S. Langley was born and raised in the North East of England, a product of Scottish, English, Scandinavian, and Western European bloodlines. His poetry is an exploration of the human condition and he has self-published a number of poetry collections including *Shadows on Hadrian's Wall* (2017), *Unbreakable Bonds* (2018) and *Snapshots* (2019) and is one of the contributing poets to *The Brampton Poetry Anthology* for both 2019 & 2020.

John lives in Cumbria and is a member of the Brampton Poetry Group through which he has participated in school poetry outreach sessions that he believes are crucially important, "enthuse the young and maturing in their ability to write, read and value poetry and you've given them a love of poetry for life," he says. John believes that poetry is a powerful means of communication and that "it is the passion and energy of the young that inspires hope and poetry can be one of their tools".

John is increasingly concerned with the lack of coordinated action in the face of human-generated climate change and believes that poetry is one of the voices through which positive change can be fostered and supported. This, his most recent collection, is his contribution to the debate.

What are you going to do now?

www.ingramcontent.com/pod-product-compliance
Lightning Source LLC
Chambersburg PA
CBHW071422270326
41914CB00042BB/2052/J